What Is a Solid?

by Jennifer Boothroyd

first step non-fiction

Lerner Books · London · New York · Minneapolis

All things are made of **matter.**

Matter is anything that takes up space.

Solid

Liquid

Gas

There are three kinds of matter.

4

A **solid** is a kind of matter.

A solid has its own shape.

Most solids do not take the
shape of their containers.

A rock is a solid. Solids can be
hard.

A toy is a solid. Solids can be soft.

A tree is a solid. Solids can be thick.

A ribbon is a solid. Solids can be thin.

Cutting a solid changes its size.

But it is still a solid.

Heating a solid can change
its shape.

Heat can change a solid into a **liquid.**

Heat can **melt** wax.

Look around. What solids do you see?

Dissolving

Some solids dissolve in water. When a solid dissolves in a liquid, it looks like the solid has disappeared. Actually, the solid has broken into very tiny pieces and mixed with the liquid. This new liquid is called a solution. The experiment on the next page is an easy way to see dissolving in action.

1. Fill a glass with hand-hot water from the tap.

2. Stir in a spoonful of sugar. Does the sugar dissolve?

3. Repeat the experiment with salt. Does salt dissolve in water?

4. Now try adding mud to a glass of water. Does that dissolve?

Solid Facts

 Some solids, like wood and wax, float in water. Other solids, like most rocks and metal, sink.

 A diamond is the hardest natural solid. People make jewellery with diamonds.

 The softest natural solid is graphite. It is the lead in pencils.

 Some solids, like dry ice, can change directly into a **gas**. They do not become liquid first.

Solids like dough and soil can take the shape of their containers. These solids need to be squished to change their shapes.

To make a chocolate bar, solid chocolate is melted. Then the liquid chocolate is poured into a container called a mould. The chocolate cools and becomes solid again. The solid chocolate keeps its new shape when it is taken out of the mould.

Glossary

 gas – something that is not a liquid and takes the shape of its container

 liquid – something that flows

 matter – anything that takes up space

 melt – to change from a solid to a liquid

 solid – something that has a definite shape

Index

The images in this book are used with the permission of: © Royalty-Free/CORBIS, pp. 2, 6, 10, 22 (middle); © Photodisc/Getty Images, pp. 3, 4 (right), 16, 22 (second from bottom); © Todd Strand/Independent Picture Service, pp. 4 (top), 5, 11, 12, 13, 22 (bottom); © Ryan McVay/Photodisc/Getty Images, p. 4 (bottom); © Erica Johnson/Independent Picture Service, pp. 7, 14; © Brendan Curran/Independent Picture Service, p. 8; © Purestock/SuperStock, p. 9; © age fotostock/SuperStock, pp. 15, 22 (second from top); USDA Photo, p. 17; © Laura Westlund/Independent Picture Service, p. 19; © Nana Twumasi/Independent Picture Service, p. 22 (top). Front Cover: © Erica Johnson/Independent Picture Service.

Illustration on page 19 by Laura Westlund/Independent Picture Service

First published in the United Kingdom in 2009 by
Lerner Books,
Dalton House,
60 Windsor Avenue,
London SW19 2RR

Website address: www.lernerbooks.co.uk

This edition was updated and edited for UK publication by Discovery Books Ltd., Unit 3, 37 Watling Street, Leintwardine, Shropshire SY7 0LW

Words in **bold** are explained in the glossary on page 22.

British Library Cataloguing in Publication Data

Boothroyd, Jennifer, 1972-
What is a solid? - (First step nonfiction. States of matter)
1. Solids - Juvenile literature
531

ISBN-13: 978 1 58013 477 4

This book was first published in the United States of America in 2007.

Printed in China